Word Garbage

A Barely Functional Anthology of Poetry

Written, compiled, edited, published,
and apologized for by
Burkshelf
(aka G.D. and Mandy Burkhead)

Word Garbage

Copyright © 2023 by Mandy and G.D. Burkhead
All Rights Reserved

Burkshelf

The characters and events in this book are fictitious. Any resemblance to persons living or dead is strictly coincidental and unintentional. This book or any portion thereof may not be reproduced, stored, transmitted, or used in any manner whatsoever without the express written permission of the authors. It is illegal to copy this book, post it to a website, or distribute it by any other means without permission.

ISBN: 978-0-9989866-9-2

Cover designed by G.D. Burkhead

"A Haiku" originally published in *Arrow Rock*, Issue 1 (2010), Lindenwood University.

"Art is Hell" originally published in *Arrow Rock*, Issue 1 (2010), Lindenwood University.

"Charity and Kindness"* originally published in *Arrow Rock*, Issue 4 (2013), Lindenwood University.

"Longing" originally published in *From a Cat's View* (2018), edited by Robin Praytor, Post-To-Print Publishers.

"My Imagination" originally published in *Tennessee's Best Emerging Poets* (2018), Z Publishing House.

"No Fabio" originally published in *Arrow Rock*, Issue 4 (2013), Lindenwood University.

*"Charity and Kindness" was inspired by the poem "Du Covoiteus et de l'Envieus" ("Mr. Greed and Mr. Envy") by Jean Bodel, translated by Nathaniel E. Dubin, *The Fabliaux* (2013), Liveright Publishing Corporation.

Table of Contents

Foreword i

Art is Hell (G.D.) 1

My Imagination (Mandy) 2

Let Free Verse Ring (G.D.) 4

Movement (G.D.) 7

Calm Before the Storm (Mandy) 8

Suchless Things (G.D.) 11

Lies (Mandy) 12

Hangin' With the Marshmallow God (G.D.) 13

An Encounter on the Appalachian
    Trail (Mandy) 16

Ode to Loss (G.D.) 18

Longing (Mandy) 20

All in Time (G.D.) 21

Beautiful (Mandy) 22

Wire Coat Hangers for Pablo Neruda (G.D.) 24

Charity and Kindness (Mandy) 26

Deadlies (G.D.) 28

Femme Fatale (Mandy) 30

"To See Better" (G.D.) 33

My Multipurpose Mind (G.D.) 34

Graffiti (Mandy)	36
Refrigerated Enlightenment (G.D.)	38
I Can't (Mandy)	39
The Rhythm (Mandy)	40
An Act of Passion (Defended) (G.D.)	42
The Miracle of Life (Mandy)	44
Dancers (Mandy)	46
The Player's Prayer (G.D.)	47
The Troll and the King (Mandy)	48
A Troll's Rebuttal (G.D.)	50
How to Wash a Kitten (Mandy)	52
Afterimage (G.D.)	55
Tough Love (Mandy)	56
With Apologies in Advance to the Billies Joel and Shakespeare (G.D.)	58
Sick Day (Mandy)	60
Negative Space (G.D.)	62
No Fabio (Mandy)	64
For Amanda (G.D.)	66
Handle with Care (Mandy)	68
A Haiku (G.D.)	70
Another Haiku (G.D.)	70

Foreword

You want to know about the pages you now clutch in your meat mittens? About us? You think we're gonna spill our life stories for you here just because you're holding our brain babies? That we're here to amuse you? Huh?

We don't roll like that, Chuckles.

Who we are matters nothing to your grasping attempt at comprehension. We are the almighty word-givers, the meaning to which meaning itself defers. Here we have crafted chaos from order and risen these poor dead tree carcasses to glory with the weight of our mindgasming. As long as you read on, your fragile sense of consciousness and perception is ours to command as we will.

You knew this when you started our little dance, you readering glutton. Don't pretend like you don't like it.

How would you even validate the knowledge we might spill upon your brainhole? This is just paper. Paper has no higher cognivities — paper do what it do and to hell with the consequences. You would trust your future understanding to paper? Sweet summer child, yes, good. Believe the sweet lies with which we wrap your innocent soul.

Yes, innocent like a virgin baby unicorn — until we blast it with the molten buckshot of our unrestrained thoughtishness! *Where is your metaphor now?*

Dear wordeater, these are not simple snippets of literary convention you will soon see set before your unprepared gazeballs; these are the labors of a fevered psyche spewing discordal musings across a blank field of expectation until imaginative wisdom blossoms and explodes inside a heart filled with gibberished longing.

Ours are seeds of freedom; you need only plant one in your head meat to let your being sprout jet turbines and cannon off into the limitless ether of enlightenization.

Run with us, friend reader; frolic gaily in the unrestrained food court of eternal wisdom, sample the godawful joy presented therein, until your mind vomits new understanding of the world as you perceive it around you. It may be just a child's party, but those are the only kind with cake anymore.

And oh, what cake we shall find ahead, *mon beret*. The cake of the gods. The cake of happiness. Cake as cake has never been caked before — *as a series of poems.*

Because when all is said and done, that's really all life is for anyone: a series of poems. Some are sweeping ballads, some are dusty limericks, and some… some are never more than haiku (Haiku! Bane of thine ink!

Why dost thou houndst me so?). But *all* deserve to be read aloud, paper-clutcher. Even the shitty ones. For if t'were not for poems, I ask you — how would we open our mics?

Let us open this mic verily and without trepidation. Leave us now, eager zenling. A journey of a thousand glances awaits you, a majestic quest through strange and exciting letters across the heralded plains of pagination.

As for us, our tasks were completed the moment you hefted this bookesque contraption. We leave you with this parting sentiment: don't ask us for our autographs, or by God, we will give them to you.

We are G.D. and Mandy Burkhead, and we have been your mind gurus.

— Burkshelf

Art is Hell
G.D. Burkhead

Dear Artist,

You will never create a masterpiece.
Your work will never be good enough.
Someone will always be better than you.
Nothing you do will ever be truly satisfying.
Everything you've accomplished could have been done better.
You will never honestly love your own creations.
No amount of training or practice will ever change this.

But if you don't tell your audience, they might not notice.

My Imagination
Mandy Burkhead

My thoughts soar
On an endless breeze.
Flipping
and spinning
and twisting
through the trees
of my imagination.
Inside my mind
is a place I escape,
to think
and feel
and be
free.

Here I have a world
of endless summer.
A world of stories
and drama and pirate's plunder.
Of mermaids singing,
and fairies dancing.
Of magical powers
and heroes romancing.

Though on the outside I may appear
calm and serene,
on the inside, I'm flying
–airborne–
carried on the wings
of my wistful dreams.

Let Free Verse Ring
G.D. Burkhead

It's really not that hard
to write poetry,
at least not the more modern kind.

All one must do is write stuff.
Write stuff down.
It doesn't
have to
rhyme
at all.

Rhythm is optional, more or less.
Try and shoot for one. It makes it sound better,
sort of,
but just so long as you're close, if
there's maybe a hint of rhythm,
if you squint your ears,
you're probably okay.

Make sure the words at least have some little thing in
common,
or at least pretend they do.

Break the sentences up here and there
from one line to the next to make it look better.

Throw in
a few
tiny
lines
now and then.

It will make it look more profound,
like you know what you're doing.

It's called free verse. I don't quite get it.
But it's popular these days with
beatniks
and the like.

Be sure to take your finished poem to a poetry club
and read it to some beatniks. They like that.
You win if they snap their fingers at you.
It means that your poem has
gained their approval.

This is the cue to feel good about yourself and maybe order one of the fancy-pants coffees they sell in places like that.

Congratulations, novice poet.
You've been accepted by the artsy-fartsy crowd.

Now go out and get yourself
a beret.
It'll make you look stylish and blend in better.

Get a black one.

Movement
G.D. Burkhead

I'm
 just
  writing
   right
    now
     because
  dancing   in
 pencil   I   my
  the   felt   hand
 feel   the   the
  motion   sudden   paper
   the   urge to   glide
    experience   beneath
              my
              fingers
           the rush of
          tiny wind as
         I scratch out
        these passing
         transient
          thoughts
           that   and
            change reshape threaten
              and   to
                          slip
                as I   pin
               even   away   them
                    entirely   down
                          beneath
                            my
                           lead

Calm Before the Storm
Mandy Burkhead

Nothing stirs,
The air is quiet,
The wind holds it breath,
The rocks anticipate.

Clouds rise on the horizon,
Dark and menacing,
Leaves hang limp with humidity,
Birds *caw, caw, caw* in warning.

Lightning strikes in the distance,
A long, sheer bolt hits the ground,
Crack! The sky splits,
Deep, grumbling, rumbling, thundering sounds.

The earth trembles beneath small feet,
Animals scamper to their dens,
Skies light up again and again,
The wind whistles through the trees,
Clothes whip, whip, around thin arms.

Run towards the house, scurry, be hasty,
Scarf snags on the branch,
Break free, flee little youngster,
Feet on gravel, *flip flop, flip flop*.

Stumble through the darkness rising,
All is calm but not for long,
Mothers wreak havoc on newly blossoming life,
Ripped from their roots, cast to the Heavens.

Hustle, bustle, scurry young tike,
The skies will undo and emit their fury,
All will be loosed upon the innocent,
Nature's dark side will be shown.

Trees lash out to suspend you,
No! Do not stumble on their bark!
Whimpering, crying daughter,
Embrace the pain and continue running.

Stand back up, young child,
Race with all your might,
The witch cackles, chuckles, giggles,
Do not let her catch you.

Almost there, almost home,
The door is right before you,
Lug, tug, shrug, the door opens,
Collapse onto the cold, dirt floor.

You're secure lass,
protected for now.
The calm has ended.
The storm will commence.

Suchless Things
G.D. Burkhead

There's no such thing as no such thing.
Everything's a thing, even the unthinged things
no one's thought yet.
Can't unthought things do things?
Is such a thing unthinkable?

Thought things with suches as are
simple, easy, predictable, thinkable;
Thingless things such as are not can do, be anything,
can surprise and excite and frighten and bite.

Verifiability bores me sometimes.
I'll have my things with no such, thanks.

Lies
Mandy Burkhead

Lies are black and white.
No grey area here.
True or false, 50/50.
Lies don't have a middle ground —
there is no part truth, part lie,
Different circumstances.
No
Take for instance or
What ifs?
There are no white lies or black lies,
all lies are the same.
False.
No "good intentions."
If what you believe is wrong, then it is a lie,
whether you believe it to be true or not.
Do you believe what I am telling you right now?
Because it is the truth.
Unless I am lying to you.

Hangin' With the Marshmallow God
G.D. Burkhead

I asked the god of marshmallows
what it was like to be
A confectionary deity,
and he replied to me:

"My priests are all quite fluffified
in thighs and gut and ass,
But nothing else can quite compare
to Toasted Mallow Mass.

We take our sacrifices
and our sacrificial rods
And take them up Mount Crispy
to insult volcano gods.

We chant and sing marshmallow songs
and dance the toasting dance
In our sacred toasting slippers
and our baggy holy pants.

The gods become quite angry
and begin to roar and cuss
And fire up their lava forge
and dump it all 'round us.

We shout for joy and gather 'round
the hot volcano mouth
And toast our sacrifices
in the fire that pours out.

Myself, I love the sweet and sav'ry
smell of smoke that rises
To me in reverent tribute
as we cook our sacrifices.

Then my mallow followers feast
on the Mallow Meal
And the crispy crunchy goodness feeds
in turn their holy zeal."

"That wasn't quite the question that I asked,"
said I to he,
"But thank you for disclosing
what you mean to do with me."

Then the god of marshmallows
smiled and proclaimed,
"Think of the joy that you will bring,
not how you will be maimed."

They stabbed me with a toasting rod
and held me on a spit
Over top of the volcano mouth
and cooked me in the pit.

My skin began to char and flake
from head to toe and back
And I became a crunchy sweet
marshmallow deity snack.

An Encounter on the Appalachian Trail
Mandy Burkhead

I came upon him
as he waddled down the trail
like a lame duck,
his back hunched,
face red,
eyebrows drawn,
sweat sticking his hair
to his head.

He was gnawing
his lower lip
as if in concentration.

A roll of cloth
was stuck in
the crack of his buttocks
and tied to his belt
in front and back
like a sumo wrestler's *kesho-mawashi*
(though he was wearing shorts underneath).

He walked with one hand
on each cheek,
spreading them wide apart.

"Whatcha doin' there, buddy?"
I asked the stranger.

"Separating the warring parties,"
he replied.

Ode to Loss
G.D. Burkhead

I sit here in my darkened room
And hold back tears of sorrow
I cannot face the world today
And probably not tomorrow

A sense of overwhelming grief
Paralyzes all my senses
And because of this most tragic loss
I'm left with no defenses

I cannot bear the thought of it
It sends me into shock
I can't believe what I have done
I've lost my favorite sock

My comfy cozy woolen sock
That warmed my toes so great
It always brightened up my day
Put me in a happy state

I wore it everywhere I went
Even in the shower
It always kept me entertained
For hour after hour

Me and my sock were bestest friends
I loved it like a brother
It was the only pal I'd need
For me, there was no other

But now my heart is very sad
My sock, it is not near
I don't know where it's located
But it sure isn't here

I wish it would come back to me
I miss it all the time
I miss it so much I can only
Think up one last rhyme

I know that I can't mope forever
So I guess that I'll make due
Since I can't find my favorite sock
I'll wear my favorite shoe

Longing
Mandy Burkhead

The cat sits before the window
staring longingly at the yard outside.

It watches the birds flitter from branch to branch,
the squirrels chasing each other around and around
tree trunks.

It sees the people pass by on the sidewalk
and lifts its rump in expectation of a good scratching.

It blinks at the bright sunlight streaming through the
clouds
and jumps nervously at a car zooming by on the
street.

With a sigh, it leaps from its perch on the window
and makes its way to a box full of sand
on the bathroom floor,
the only real dirt its feet will ever sink into,
and it cries to itself because
all it ever wanted
was to shit outside.

All in Time
G.D. Burkhead

I lay in bed, and the only thing I can hear
Is the rhythmic *tock, tock, tock* of time
Murmuring through my roommate's clock.
The only way I can see
Is by the small red glare of time
As it stares at me through my own alarm clock.
The only reason I sense anything at all
Is because time helps me,
Allows me.
All I see and hear and feel is time,
And I wonder,

If we smashed every clock in the world,
Would time still exist?
Would we?

Beautiful
Mandy Burkhead

When the thunder groans
through my bones

like the rolling
of a drum

before the dive
in a circus act

and the lightning crackles
through the thick
blanket of heavy air

briefly illuminating
my sight,
so bright it hurts
my eyes

before plunging me
into darkness,

and on top of it all
the rain echoes

through my room
with a metallic
cling

in conjunction
with the wind's whistle,

making my curtain billow
like the gown of a Greek goddess,

then, I am most
at peace.

Wire Coat Hangers for Pablo Neruda
G.D. Burkhead

I wake up and
they clang against my head as I pull down my wool
sweater with the gray fuzz and copper noise
they beat a tattoo cacophony and twinkle like hoarse
vultures squawking
beautifully through my skull in the dim sludge of
sunrise underground

I wake up and
bronze knots clap and scream in protestation at the
action of
life anew disturbing cotton silence in faraway crannies
Beelzebub's triangles in a hellish orchestra of
unwanted consciousness saying
back to Oblivion sentience is pain and

I agree, but
it's the damned brass band that assaults my senses
and
stabs echoing nails into my new membrane and

Life is not always
alarmist sirens warning of hurt and futility and
the traitorous voices whispering false sophistry

Living is actually
quite pleasant.

I only hate the harpies.
And I will rise to spite them.

Charity and Kindness
(Based on the poem "Mr. Greed and Mr. Envy" by
Jean Bodel)
Mandy Burkhead

Greed and Envy were put to the test
Saint Martin offered a favor
"Whoever asks first gets his wish.
Whoever doesn't, I will dish
Out double to him what the first one got."

Greed wanted everything for himself
and would not go first—
Envy could not stand the thought
that Greed would get more than he got.

Eventually a consensus was reached
Envy wished to lose an eye
and Greed lost twice.
In the end, both were blind.

Saint Martin then came upon
Greed and Envy's opposites: Charity and Kindness.
Saint Martin put them also to the test
offering the same deal.

Charity, ever sacrificial,
offered to let Kindness choose second.
But Kindness could not stand the thought
of his brother having less than he got.

Neither could be bought.
Until dawn they gently conspired
neither willing to receive after the other
and Saint Martin left without bestowing a gift,
thinking to himself that
at least Greed and Envy had got
something for their lot.

Deadlies
G.D. Burkhead

Pride climbs to the top of the tower,
Her purple robes shining in the sun,
Cries, "Here I am!" then swan dives from the peak.

Wrath screams across the barren cliff face,
Battle scarred in bloody battered armor,
Draws his sword and leaps over the edge.

Lust splays out across the silken sheets,
Naked from the chin down, her face painted,
Her hips buck once, then she falls asleep.

Sloth just sits inside the empty room,
Wrapped in a towel, more like a shroud, a blanket,
Lays back his head, and sighs, and drifts away.

Gluttony reaches fat fingers across the table,
Skin rolls forward, stained cloak dips in sauce,
He gasps, then falls into his plate.

Envy grips the wall and hides behind,
Eyes sharp, silk dress tattered, frayed,
Glares daggers at the world, then slits her wrists.

Greed lounges in his private office suite,
Cigar smoke billowing, suit not tight enough,
And grumbles as his hoard comes crashing down.

Seven sins, all deadly, self-destructive,
All sculptors of the heart and mind and soul,
Their cursed gifts eternally renewed.

Each has a role in suffering to play,
But if they left, how boring would we be?
And without them, what worth does virtue hold?

Femme Fatale
Mandy Burkhead

She haunts you with her beauty
her infinite grace
her seductive body
her eloquent face.

Her blood red hair
falls down her bare back
it turns every head
stops them in their tracks.

She draws you in with her eyes
mysterious and dark;
the contrast to her ivory skin
is incredibly stark.

Her crimson lips
sweet as a rose
make your body stiffen
when they draw close.

Her curvy body
and ample bust
when pressed against you
make you sweat with lust.

And that tantalizing voice
husky and sly
"You've been a bad boy,
and now you must die."

And out of the darkness
plunges a dagger
into your chest
you gasp and you stagger.

You fall to the ground
blood covers your hand
you stare up in shock
as above you she stands.

She throws back her head
a manic laugh leaves her lips
and she licks your blood
off her fingertips.

"You've been ordered assassinated
by the Children of Death
I hope that you suffer
to your last breath."

She dons her crimson gown
her black cloak and hood
and disappears into the night
from whence she stood.

You close your eyes
and see her face
and the curves of her body
in your mind you trace.

For even in death
she is captivating
the femme fatale
lives for the killing.

"To See Better"
G.D. Burkhead

"You're not allowed to make things up," he said.

That is a sad,
sad sentence to hear, especially
from an art teacher. All of our
projects, then, must be
copies
of something else. No
new material, no
new thoughts, no
new ideas will be tolerated;
we are only here to
repeat
what was already done. The
greatest artists, then, must be
color copiers.

Well.

What a relief to know that
my imagination is
unnecessary.

My Multipurpose Mind
G.D. Burkhead

My mind is a fist
That beats my body into submission
And leaves bruises on the flesh of my life

My mind is a flamethrower
That burns away the blankness on the page
And leaves only beautiful ashes

My mind is a poison
That slips down the throats, eyes, ears of all I meet
And slowly chokes the thoughts that aren't like mine

My mind is a hammer
That slams against the molten world around me
And forges it into a shape I like

My mind is a cannon
That blasts my consciousness into imagination
And sends it screaming through the other side

My mind is a boot
That stomps the scurrying roaches of ignorance
And grinds the life out of them into the dirt

My mind is a volcano
That blasts my molten creativity into the sky
And rains flaming masterpieces on the land

My mind is a machine gun
That fires rattling thoughts into innocent crowds
And mows them down in a hail of genius

My mind is a meteor
That careens through the void of history
And with my legacy annihilates convention

My mind is a fuzzy dandelion petal
That lists with millions of others on a gentle breeze
And drifts slowly ever onward, far as it can float

Graffiti
Mandy Burkhead

From ancient caverns
To rustic taverns
(Since the beginning of human history)

On bathroom stalls
And brick walls
(No place is safe)

Murals of peni in Pompei
Names carved in a tree
(We were never very clever)

So-and-so was here
If your reading this your queer
(And always terrible with grammar)

She's a nasty slut
Homos take it up the butt
(Quite obsessed with fornication)

Sex with a nine
Call for a good time
(Always seeking human connection)

Fight the system
Learn to shut up and listen
(Profound? Sometimes)

I had sex on this toilet seat
This bathroom smells like cats in heat
(Disturbing? Often)

The essence of human need
Screaming out loud "Notice me!"
(Proof of existence — but nobody cares)

Refrigerated Enlightenment
G.D. Burkhead

The sound my refrigerator makes
Is the sound of the universe
Humming beneath my bed
Like the tinkling of distant stars
Whispering the secrets of eternity
To leftover pizza.

I always knew there was something transcendental
in that cheese.

I Can't
Mandy Burkhead

I can't whistle
or quirk an eyebrow
or blow a bubble
from a wad of gum.
I can't sing on key
or cook perfect crêpes
or pee standing up.
I can't exercise
without hurting
or walk in heels
without falling
or drink alcohol
without grimacing.
I can't always keep a plant alive
or keep on top of my homework
or keep myself from getting
too stressed out.

But dammit don't you try and stop me.

The Rhythm
Mandy Burkhead

The waves roll rhythmically
into the soft, warm sand.

The smell of salt
and sweat
hangs in the air.

A gasp
as the fingers
of warm water
brush against tender skin.

In the moonlight
two bodies meet
one hard and strong
one soft and yielding.

The shells tumble
in the waves
as the tide rises.

The sea steadily thrusts
its will upon the bank, until
with a *crash*
the sea sprays
against the rocks.

The water retreats,
the ocean calms,
the wind dies down.

All is quiet for a moment.
Then the rhythm begins anew.

An Act of Passion (Defended)
G.D. Burkhead

Long and rigid, firm and strong
(My audience will read this wrong)

Caress the shaft, breathe in, breathe out
(No, that's not what it's about)

Start out slow, then pick up speed
(It's not that way, it's not that deed)

Panting, straining, dripping sweat
(Please don't get excited yet)

Grabbing, thrusting, arching back
(I swear, it's really not like that)

Ram it in, the tension mounts
(It's really tame by all accounts)

Shove, releasing, soaring high
(I'm not that crude, I'm not "that guy")

Writhing, squirming, climax now
(This poem's tasteful, you'll see how)

Peaking, falling, drifting down
(I can explain, just stick around)

Breathing ragged, laying spent
(We all can tell where your mind went)

Wrapped in softness, throbbing heart
(It's not obscene, it's really art)

Roll off and stand on trembling legs
("What's it *about*?" the reader begs)

A perfect moment, how exalting
(There's nothing else quite like pole vaulting)

The Miracle of Life
Mandy Burkhead

Women have told me
how beautiful it is to give birth.

To carry around a child for nine months
your stomach and breasts swelling
your nipples secreting milk
losing control of your bladder whenever
you laugh or sneeze.

Then, when the baby comes
water gushes from between your legs
and your vagina dilates to
the size of a bowling ball
stretching like a rubber band.

The baby comes out
covered in blood and mucus;
they have to suck the liquid
out of its nose and mouth
so it can breathe.

In some cultures,
women dry the umbilical cord

and use it as a talisman
to ward off evil.

In America, where anything
can be sold for consumption,
there are hair and facial care products with
placenta mixed in.

And then, when you take your
little bundle of joy home
you get to stay up all night with it
while it cries, and wallows in its own filth,
and pukes on you if you so much as
bounce it on your knee.

And now it's your duty
as a parent, to make sure
you don't somehow accidentally
end up killing the thing.

They tell me it is beautiful
to give birth, to raise a child.

But as for me, I think I'll
just skip the whole
"miracle of life" thing.

Dancers
Mandy Burkhead

Glitter

Vivid colors
Shiny sequins
Soft skin, exposed
In the brilliant stage lights

The vibration of music
The swirl of colors
As the dancers begin to move
Bright smiles on their faces

A kaleidoscope of images
Individuals blend into one
A strong, rich voice begins to sing
Stealing the spotlight

Mesmerizing bodies move in graceful harmony
Dancing, bending, twirling, jumping
To the rhythm of the music
And the crowd's applause

The Player's Prayer
G.D. Burkhead

Our developer who art online,
Epic be thy game.
Thy autosave load.
I level up
At home as on the servers.
Give us this session our daily quests,
And forgive us our camping,
As we forgive those who camp against us,
And lead us not into cheese strats,
But deliver us from glitches.
"You Win."

The Troll and the King
Mandy Burkhead

There once was a Troll.
When he stomped into a village
the people fled and hid in their homes.
He was a crude creature,
drunken and slovenly.
He gnashed his teeth
and emitted foul odors.
When he was around
the villagers had to be careful what they said
for he was quick to fits of rage,
of threats, and of breaking things.

There was a King, too.
He wore a crown atop his graying head.
There were lines around his eyes from laughter,
and his smile took up his whole face.
Adventurous and kind, he was a friend to all.
But if you looked closely,
sometimes, briefly,
you might catch a glimpse
of a tear in his eye
when he reminisced on the fate of his kingdom.

The Troll and the King
were locked in eternal battle,
though many couldn't see it.
They were evenly matched,
and at the end of each day
one might win against the other
and think his adversary defeated.
But they would both return the next dawn
to begin the fight again.
And the people of the kingdom remained
caught in the middle.

A Troll's Rebuttal
G.D. Burkhead

Meat people say, "Troll is dumb."
But troll is not dumb!
Troll just think slower.
Troll not in hurry all time like meat people.
Troll sit and watch glacier stampede across countryside,
Laugh at mountain dancing together in conga line—
But meat people in too big hurry appreciate geography.
Meat people is dumb.

Meat people say, "Troll is ugly."
But troll is not ugly!
Troll beauty all natural.
Troll not need cover body with gunk like meat people.
Troll know each troll strong and unique,
Thread with vein of bright malachite or shimmering hematite or calico sediment—
But meat people too self-conscious appreciate geology.
Meat people is ugly.

Meat people say, "Troll is mean."
But troll is not mean!
Troll very in touch with earth.
Troll not mutilate and steal from planet like meat people.
Troll friend with plant thing and meat creature,
Only take what need and put back when done —
But meat people too greedy appreciate ecology.
Meat people is mean.

Meat people say, "Troll is tough."
And yes, troll is very tough!
Troll skin harder than boulder.
Troll not squishy and easily smushed like meat people.
Troll has molten rock for blood and diamond for teeth,
Crunch granite like meat people crunch plant food —
Meat people not too dumb appreciate this.
Meat people is not tough.

Maybe meat people try not be dumb and ugly and mean too?
Troll appreciate very much, thanks.

How to Wash a Kitten
Mandy Burkhead

First, rescue your kittens
from the hoarder down the street
who abandoned two of them
in front of her house
in the pouring rain
with no food or water.

Take your two little kittens
back to your house
and throw away their cat carrier
and the statue of a horse
that was in there for companionship
or some such shit.

After feeding your starving kittens
a mixture of cat food and milk,
take one kitten at a time
and gently lower it
into a bucket of soapy water
hold on tight
as it squirms and tries to escape.

(Oh right, you'll be wanting to
Wear gloves for this part.)
Now scrub your kitten
with the flea soap
starting from tail to head.

Have a friend hold the kitten
while you pick the fleas off
one by one with a pair of tweezers.

Reach the head and realize
that all the fleas are now
in the kitten's eyes and ears.
Finish removing the fleas
and rinse your unhappy kitten.

Follow the same steps for kitten two
but this time
go from head to tail
with the flea soap.

Dry your kittens
until they turn into
little balls of fluff.

Then throw out your water
and scrub yourself furiously
from head to toe
in the shower
as you are now also
covered in fleas,
dirty kitten mud,
and scratches from
those cute little bastards.

Now go find your little kittens
all fluffy and clean
and hold them
while they fall asleep
in your lap, weary
from the day's activities.

Afterimage
G.D. Burkhead

As I turn off the light, for a split second,
I see a flash of green over my skin.
A phantom me, hiding beneath myself,
who sees his chance and escapes into the night.

When I turn the light back on,
I'm blinded for a moment.
That must be when
he sneaks back in.

Tough Love
Mandy Burkhead

My children are killing me.

I birthed them from my womb,
nourished them with my own body.
I gave them everything.
but still they wanted more.

They have become a cancer.
Slowly growing and growing, taking me over.
I am not what I once was
when I first conceived them.

My once lush, nubile body
is decaying, filled with tumors,
disease seeping from my pores.

My youthful vitality
has been stripped away.
I am sick all the time now;
a raging fever consumes me.

Each day, I find it harder to breathe.

I know that it is not their fault;
it is in their nature
to consume all that they see
to grow and spread.
After all, I created them.

But I also know that I must survive
even if it means that they do not.
Whether by burning, or drenching, or blowing,
starvation or dehydration.
If all else fails, I will freeze them off.

I must carve out this disease
and free myself
for my own sake
and for theirs. The ones who survive.

My children are killing me.

As much as it hurts me to do so,
I must kill them first.

With Apologies in Advance to the Billies Joel and Shakespeare

(To be read to the tune of "Piano Man" by Billy Joel)

G.D. Burkhead

When Julius Caesar beat Pompey
Oh, what a party Rome had
But Marullus and Flavius, and also Cassius
Were jealous and angry and sad

So Cassius told Brutus, "Let's kill the guy"
But Brutus said, "Give me some time
"I'll do it if Rome really wants me to
"But first, we must speak in rhyme"

So Cassius sends Brutus fake letters
That convince him to join in the game
But his wife goes all crazy, and the next day,
We see Calphurnia does the same

But somehow they get Caesar to the Senate
With their daggers, they stab him a lot
"*Et tu, Brute?*" he cries, then soon after dies
Oh, and happy Marc Antony's not

At the funeral, Brutus tells the plebeians
From the ambitious Caesar, they're free
And since Caesar was bad that means everyone's glad
At least for a minute or three

But then Antony delivers his eulogy
And the plebeians, they get really sore
So they chase the conspirators outta town
Cuz now they like Antony more

Now Rome has got a new triumvirate
Since Octavius Caesar's in town
And they gather up some men, and head out again
To hunt Brutus and Cassius down

They catch up to 'em finally in Philippi
A terrible battle ensues
Both conspirators run themselves through and die
Once they realize that they're gonna lose

Oh, give us a play, Roman Caesar man!
Give us a play tonight
Everyone who killed you got killed in the end
That's what you'd call tragic alright

Sick Day
Mandy Burkhead

She snivels and snorts,
then gives up,
taking a tissue and blowing her nose.

Her cheeks are flushed
her nose bright red
her eyes watering.

When she sneezes
the mixture of snot and spit
gets on her face and hands
and even in her hair.

Her breath smells like
cough drops and medicine,
and when she talks
her voice is nasally.

She tells me she doesn't want
to get out of bed this morning
as she sits with the covers pulled up to her chin
a graveyard of tissues on the floor around her.

She looks miserable and pathetic
as she pulls herself out of the bed anyway
to get ready for the day.

Wrapping my arms around her,
I kiss her on the forehead and tell her that
she has never looked more adorable.

Negative Space
G.D. Burkhead

The fact that you're another person is

      excruciating.

That means that I'll never be as

      close to you

as I want to be, which is

closer than I am

to myself.

Whenever we hug, it's

      a lie;

it's just me trying to pretend

we're one being.

I loathe the air between us, the

        space

that defines

        you

like I wish I could.

It's not fair —

it doesn't know you like I do.

What right does it have, then, to

always be so

        near?

No Fabio
Mandy Burkhead

You are no Fabio —
your muscleless chest,
rounded belly,
and pale skin
will never grace the cover
of a romance novel.

Your hair is not long and silky
and does not flow well in a breeze.

The skin of your face is naturally oily
your scalp flakes with dandruff
you wear glasses over your dark eyes
that are not at all like cerulean orbs.

Your knees are bony,
your hands are veiny,
your toes are freakishly long.

You are tall,
but you slouch down when you stand
as if your height is awkward to you,
and you cannot dance.

No, you are no Fabio,
but I never much cared for Fabio anyway.

You are still my Highlander,
my Elven Warrior,
Noble Pirate, Untamable Rogue,
Stranger in the Moonlight,
and Laird for All Time.

But most importantly
you are mine.

For Amanda
G.D. Burkhead

How do I even begin to describe what you do to me?
No word, no thought can do it justice.

Were I to paint a thousand pictures
to hold a million words,
not one could touch you.
Not one could come close to expressing
how I feel for you.

A billion words of love in a million images of you is
still not enough,
still too meager.

My only apology is that you can never have an inkling
of what you really mean,
because the world is not enough to allow me to
express it.

So instead of a thousand,
A million,
A billion,

I offer you three,
which is as good as any more in comparison to the untouchable truth.

And those three pathetic gifts,
the best I can give,
are these:

I love you.

Handle with Care
Mandy Burkhead

This is not a toy.

Do not leave out in the rain.

Do not drop.

Hand wash in warm
soapy water only.

Be patient when awakening
from sleep mode.

Do not overheat.

If a fire occurs,
shut the door and wait
for the fire to extinguish.

If the fire does not
extinguish on its own,
do not attempt to do so yourself
without proper precautions.

Do not attempt to turn on
without warming up first.

Do not unplug while in use.

If used improperly
a breakdown may occur.

It is your responsibility
to fix if broken.

If you treat gently
and use properly
you are ensured
a lifetime guarantee.

A Haiku
G.D. Burkhead

This is a haiku.
    It's friggin' poetic, y'all.
        You know you want it.

Another Haiku
G.D. Burkhead

Haiku! Oh shit! Cool!
    But I don't give half a damn:
        Fuck this haiku (please).

About Burkshelf

Mandy and G.D. Burkhead (who goes by either Gary or Dan, take your pick) are a married author couple responsible for *The Black Lily*, *A Single Spark*, *The Queen's Runner* (under their penname D.B. Francais), and now this weird collection of lyrical nonsense you're currently holding. Sorry about that.

The two first met in high school in a writing chatroom, where they fell in love while working on their first story together. That story would turn out to be a barely functioning mess not suitable for print, but they got better over time and eventually started publishing the good shit. They know what they're doing now, promise.

The poets(?) now live in Tennessee with their dog and three cats, all of whom dutifully keep the carpets absolutely covered in animal hair and little bits of kibble that somehow got away from them and went on little kibble adventures under the furniture.

When they aren't working or writing (Mandy and G.D., that is, the animals are useless), they enjoy reading, playing video games, cosplaying, attending conventions, and generally nerding out. Stop by their house and ask to play a boardgame; they'll very likely agree after being weirded out for a moment. Or ask Mandy about the flowers in her garden and hang onto your butt while she gives you a free lecture about the importance of pollinator-friendly native plants.

They're also down for a good D&D campaign, if anyone's asking. Just throwing that out there.

Hey, follow them online, maybe? It couldn't hurt. They can't do you any more harm than they already have, at least.

Website: www.burkshelf.com
Facebook, Twitter, Instagram: @burkshelf

www.ingramcontent.com/pod-product-compliance
Lightning Source LLC
Chambersburg PA
CBHW030456010526
44118CB00011B/966